THOMAS CRANE LIBRARY
QUINCY MA

CITY APPROPRIATION

What Do Animals Do in Winter?

How Animals Survive the Cold

By Melvin and Gilda Berger
Illustrated by Susan Harrison

Ideals Children's Books • Nashville, Tennessee

a.s.

12.00

E

The authors, artist, and publisher wish to thank the following for their invaluable advice and instruction for this book:

Jane Hyman, B.S., M.Ed. (Reading), M.Ed. (Special Needs), C.A.E.S. (Curriculum, Administration, and Supervision)

Rose Feinberg, B S., M.Ed. (Elementary Education), Ed.D. (Reading and Language Arts)

R.L. 2.3 Spache

Text copyright © 1995 by Melvin and Gilda Berger
Illustrations copyright © 1995 by Hambleton-Hill Publishing, Inc.

All rights reserved. No part of this publication may be reproduced or transmitted in any form or by any means, electronic or mechanical, including photocopy, recording, or any information storage and retrieval system, without permission in writing from the publisher.

Published by Ideals Children's Books
An imprint of Hambleton-Hill Publishing, Inc.
Nashville, Tennessee 37218

J
E
591.5
BER

Printed and bound in Mexico

Library of Congress Cataloging-in-Publication Data
Berger, Melvin.
What do animals do in winter? : how animals survive the cold / by Melvin and Gilda Berger ; illustrated by Susan Harrison.
p. cm.—(Discovery readers)
Includes index.
ISBN 1-57102-055-1 (lib. bdg.)—ISBN 1-57102-041-1 (paper)
1. Animals—Wintering—Juvenile literature. [1. Animals—Wintering. 2. Winter.] I. Berger, Gilda. II. Harrison, Susan J., ill. III. Title. IV. Series.
QL753.B37 1995
591.54'3—dc20 95-10419
CIP
AC

What Do Animals Do in Winter? is part of the *Discovery Readers*™ series.
Discovery Readers is a trademark of Hambleton-Hill Publishing, Inc.

In winter some places turn very cold.
Icy winds blow.
The trees have no leaves.
The flowers are gone.
Ponds freeze over.
Snow covers the ground.
And most animals are missing.

What do the animals *do* when it gets very cold?

Animals travel.

Some animals migrate (MI-grate).
That means they leave their homes
and travel to other places.
They go to places
—where the weather is warm
—where they can find food.
Here they stay until spring.

In spring the animals return home.
The weather is warm now.
Everything is starting to grow again.
The animals stay here until winter
comes.
Then they migrate again.

Some kinds of birds migrate.
They know when it's time to go.
The weather turns chilly.
The days grow shorter.

The birds gather together.
They sit in groups on telephone
wires and in trees.
Soon they are ready to fly away.
Off they go.

Some birds fly far away.
Other birds go only a short distance.

Robins migrate.
But they do not go very far.
They go just far enough to find food.

Other birds go much farther.
Warblers fly over 2,000 miles.

The Arctic tern migrates the farthest.
This seabird lives near the North Pole.
In winter it flies 11,000 miles south.
Finally it reaches the South Pole.
In spring it flies all the way back.

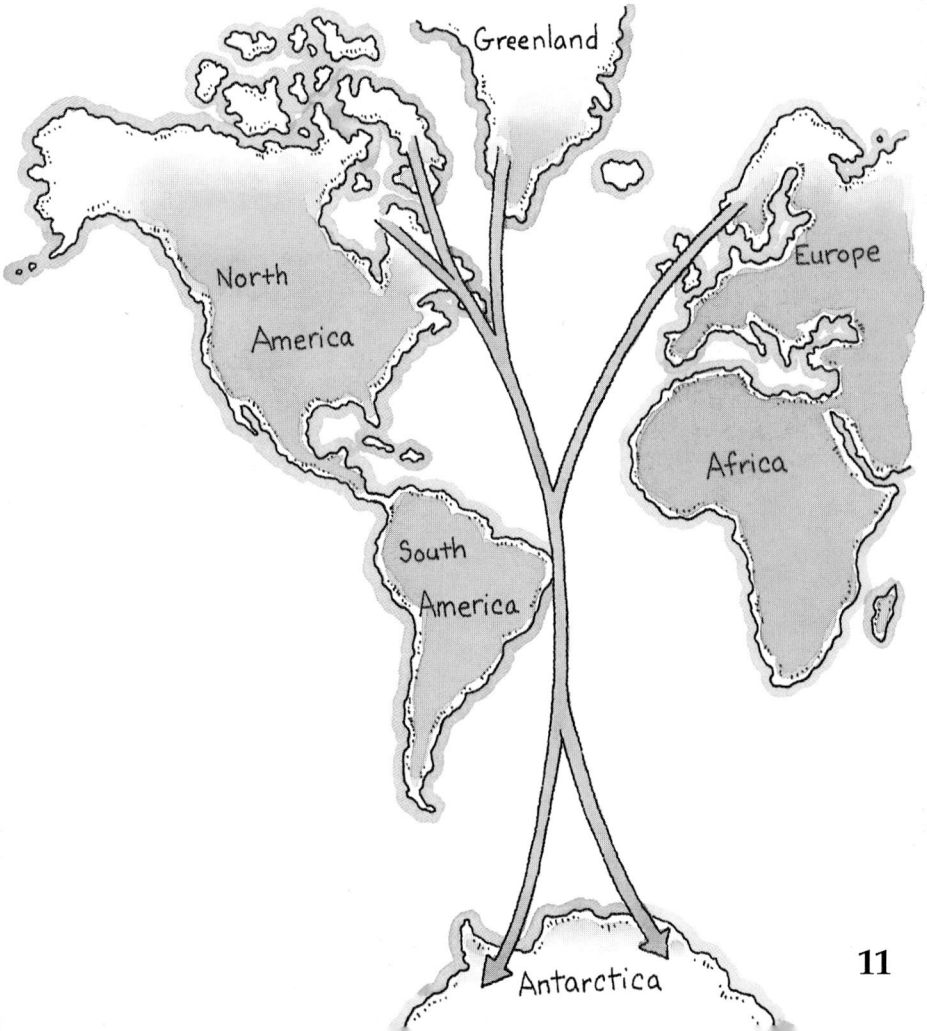

Monarch (MON-ark) butterflies live
in Canada.
They also go south in winter.
But first they must get ready.
In fall they gather in huge numbers.
Then they fly away.

Some fly to Florida.
Some fly to California.
Some fly as far south as Mexico.

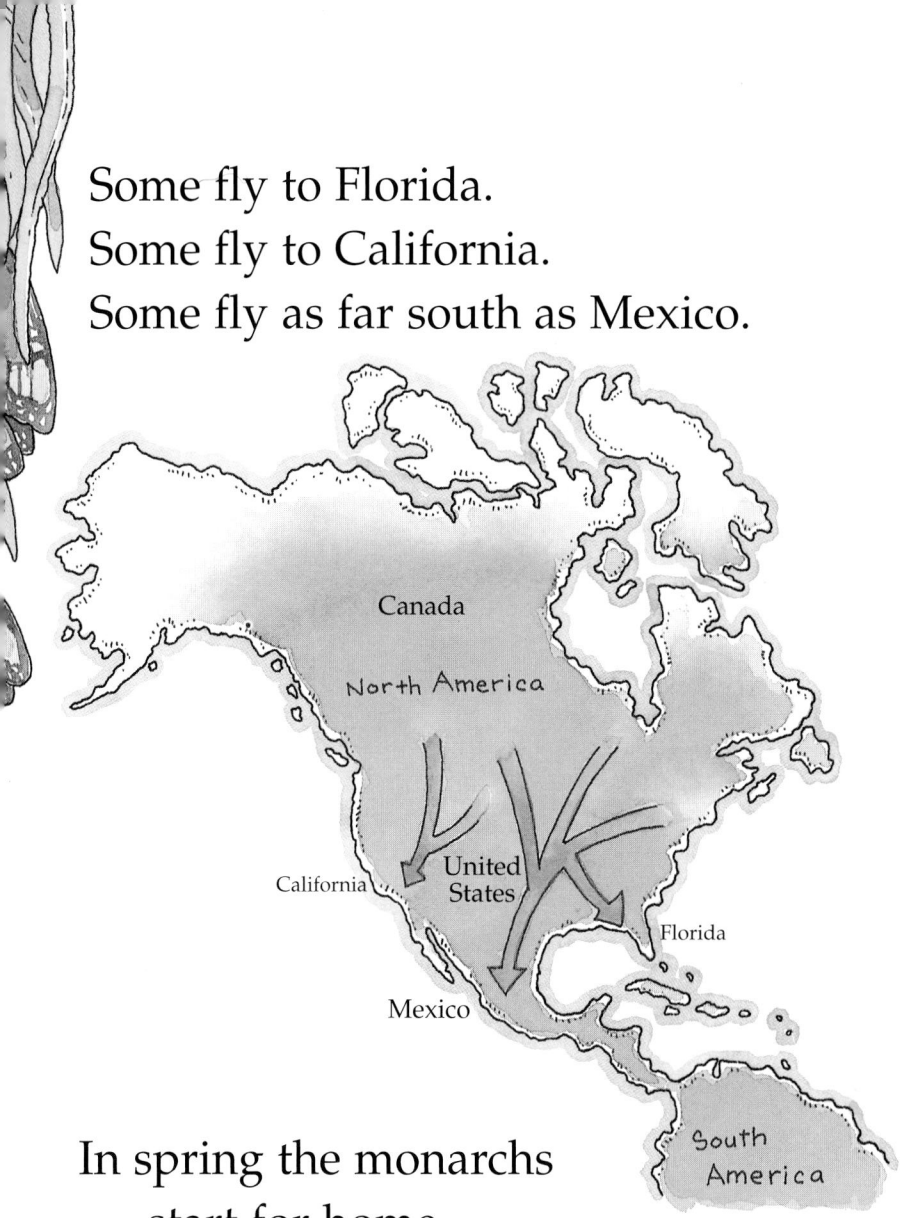

In spring the monarchs
start for home.
Along the way they lay eggs and die.
Soon the eggs hatch.
The new butterflies finish the trip.

Reindeer (RAIN-deer) live in cold lands.
Some live on mountains.
In winter the snow piles up.
It buries the grasses and leaves.
The reindeer have little to eat.

Each year the reindeer migrate.
Thousands may travel together.
They go to places with less snow.

They go into valleys.
There they find plants to eat.
They go back home in the spring.

Some whales live in cold ocean
waters.
There's lots to eat here.
But in winter the waters freeze over.
So the whales migrate.

The whales go to warmer waters.
The mothers have their babies.
By spring the young whales have grown quite big.
They swim back home with their mothers.

What *else* do animals do when it gets very cold?

Animals sleep.

Some animals hibernate (HI-bur-nate)
in winter.
That means they go to sleep.
They find places
—where they can stay warm
—where they will feel safe.

Groundhogs hibernate in winter.
They sleep in nests.
Their nests are inside tunnels under
the ground.

All spring and summer the
groundhogs are busy.
They eat and eat.
They find plants and grass
everywhere.
Soon they are big and fat.

In fall the groundhogs get ready to hibernate.
They line their nests with grass.
Then they curl up.
They wrap their tails around themselves.
And they go to sleep for the winter.

Groundhogs may sleep for six months.
They do not eat.
They live off the fat in their bodies.
They lose about half of their weight.

In spring the groundhogs come out of their tunnels.
They look around for food.
The males and females mate.
Four weeks later, baby groundhogs are born.

Bats also hibernate.
But they hibernate in caves.
They hang upside down.
They wrap their wings around themselves.
That keeps them warm while they sleep.

Frogs and turtles hibernate too.
So do snakes, snails, and some kinds of squirrels.
These animals lie very still.
They breathe slowly.
They grow cold and stiff.
And they don't eat anything all winter.

turtle

snail

snake

frog

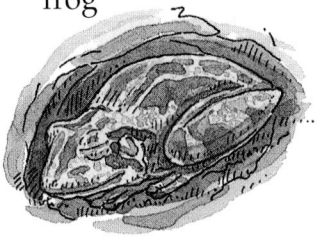

Bears hibernate in caves or in holes in the ground.
But they are light sleepers.
They may wake to look for food.
Then they go back to sleep.

Raccoons also sleep through the cold winters.
They make their dens in hollow trees, logs, or stumps.
On warmer days, they might wake up and look for food.
Then they go back to their dens.

Chipmunks are light sleepers too.
All spring and summer they gather food.
They store it in tunnels under the ground.

In fall the chipmunks get ready for winter.
They cover the food with dried grass.
The dried grass is their bed.
They climb on top and go to sleep.

In winter the chipmunks wake once in a while.
They are hungry.
So they reach under their bed for a snack.
Then they go back to sleep.

What *else* do animals do when it gets very cold?

Animals hide.

Some animals hide in winter.
They hide in their dens or nests.
Here they keep warm.

Some kinds of squirrels hide in
winter.

Sometimes the squirrels come out.
They look for something to eat.
Often they are lucky.
They find the nuts they hid in fall.
They find the food people put in
feeders.

Bees hide in their hives in winter.
Honeybees pile up in one big ball.
The center ones wiggle to keep warm.
The outside ones push their way inside.
The bees eat the honey they made in the summer.
On warm days some fly out to find more food.

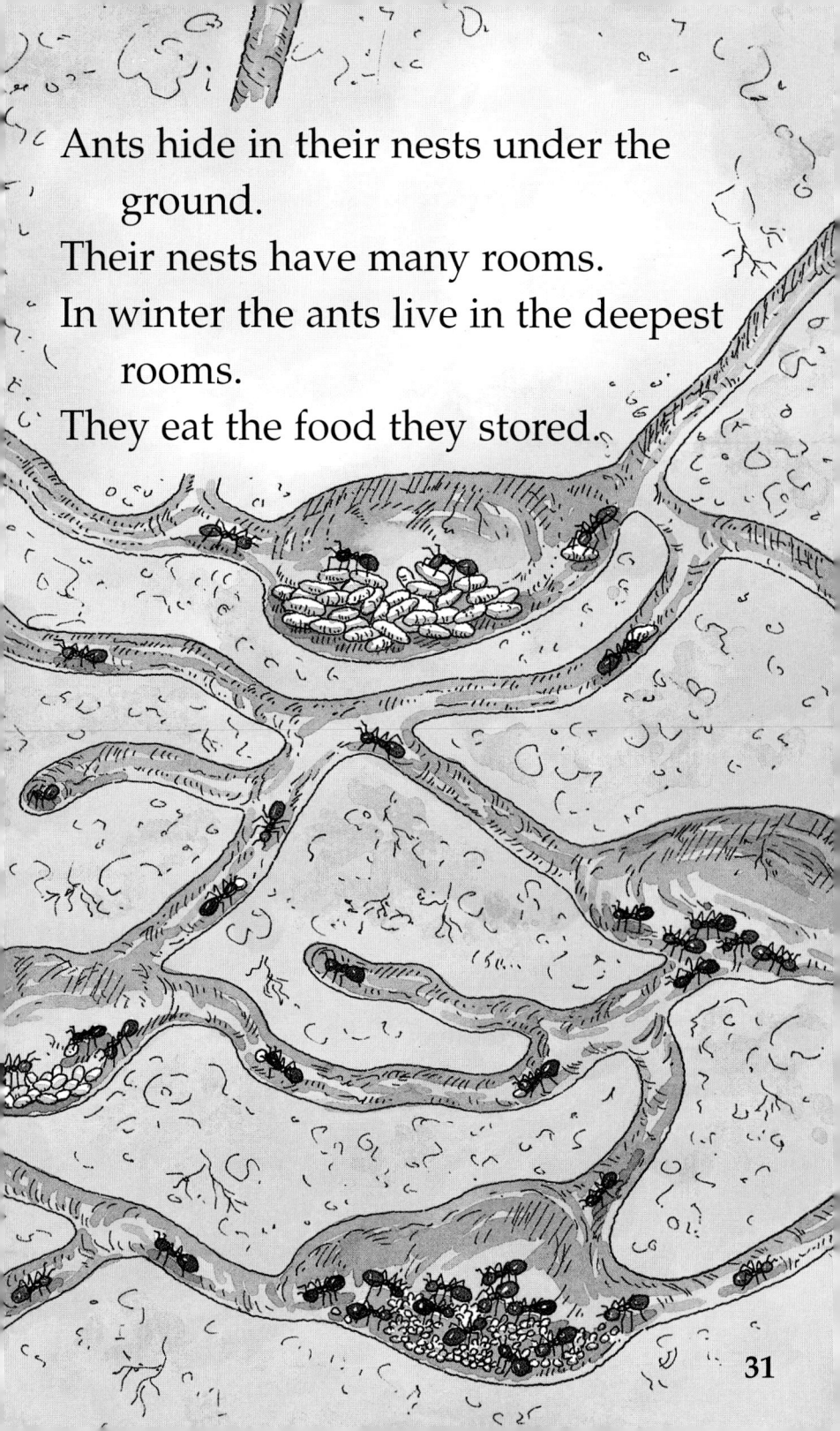

Ants hide in their nests under the ground.
Their nests have many rooms.
In winter the ants live in the deepest rooms.
They eat the food they stored.

Beavers hide in their lodges.
Lodges are houses that beavers build.
The houses are above the water.
They are warm and dry.

All summer the beavers are busy.
They cut down trees with their teeth.
They store the pieces inside their lodges.

In winter the beavers stay inside.
They eat the bark from the wood they stored.

lodge

Caterpillars (KAT-uh-pil-urs) make houses called cocoons.
The cocoons hang from branches.
The caterpillars stay warm and dry inside.

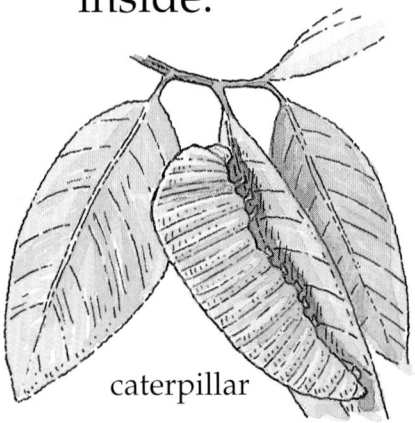
caterpillar

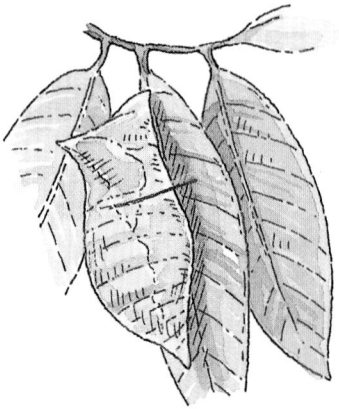
cocoon

In spring they come out as butterflies.

butterfly

Crickets are leaping insects.
In fall they lay their eggs in the ground and then die.
All winter the eggs stay in the ground.
In spring the eggs hatch.
Tiny baby crickets come out.

What *else* do animals do when it gets very cold?

Animals change color.

Some animals change color.
This helps them hide from other animals.

Weasels are small furry animals.
In summer they have brown fur.
It is hard to see them on the ground.
In fall the weasels get ready for winter.
The color of their fur changes.
Their brown fur turns white.
The white fur helps hide the weasel in the snow.

Snowshoe rabbits change their fur color.
Most of the year they are brown.
But in winter they grow coats of white fur.

A bird called a ptarmigan (TAR-mi-gun) also changes its color.
Most of the time its feathers are brown and black.
But in winter its feathers turn white.
The white feathers hide the bird in the snow.

Foxes don't hibernate.
They don't migrate.
They don't hide.
Most don't change color.
What do *they* do when it gets very cold?

In winter foxes grow extra fur.
The fur traps air.
The layer of air keeps the foxes warm.
All winter the foxes hunt as usual.
They catch mice, chickens, rabbits,
and birds.

Here's a surprise.
In different parts of the world, it is cold at different times of the year.
In some places it is cold in December.
In other places it is cold in July.

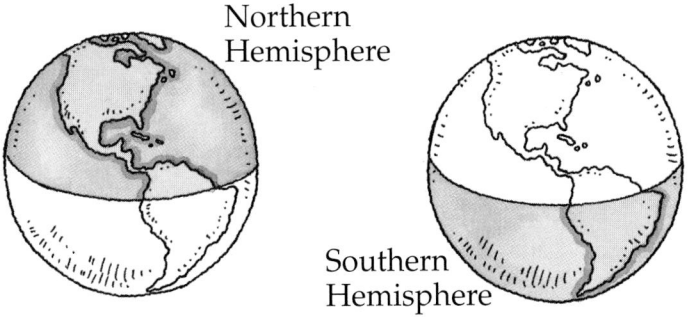

The earth is divided into two parts.
The top part is called the Northern Hemisphere.
Some places here have winter weather from December to early March.

The bottom part of the earth is called the Southern Hemisphere.
Some places here have winter weather from late June to early September.

The green areas on this map are warm all year round.

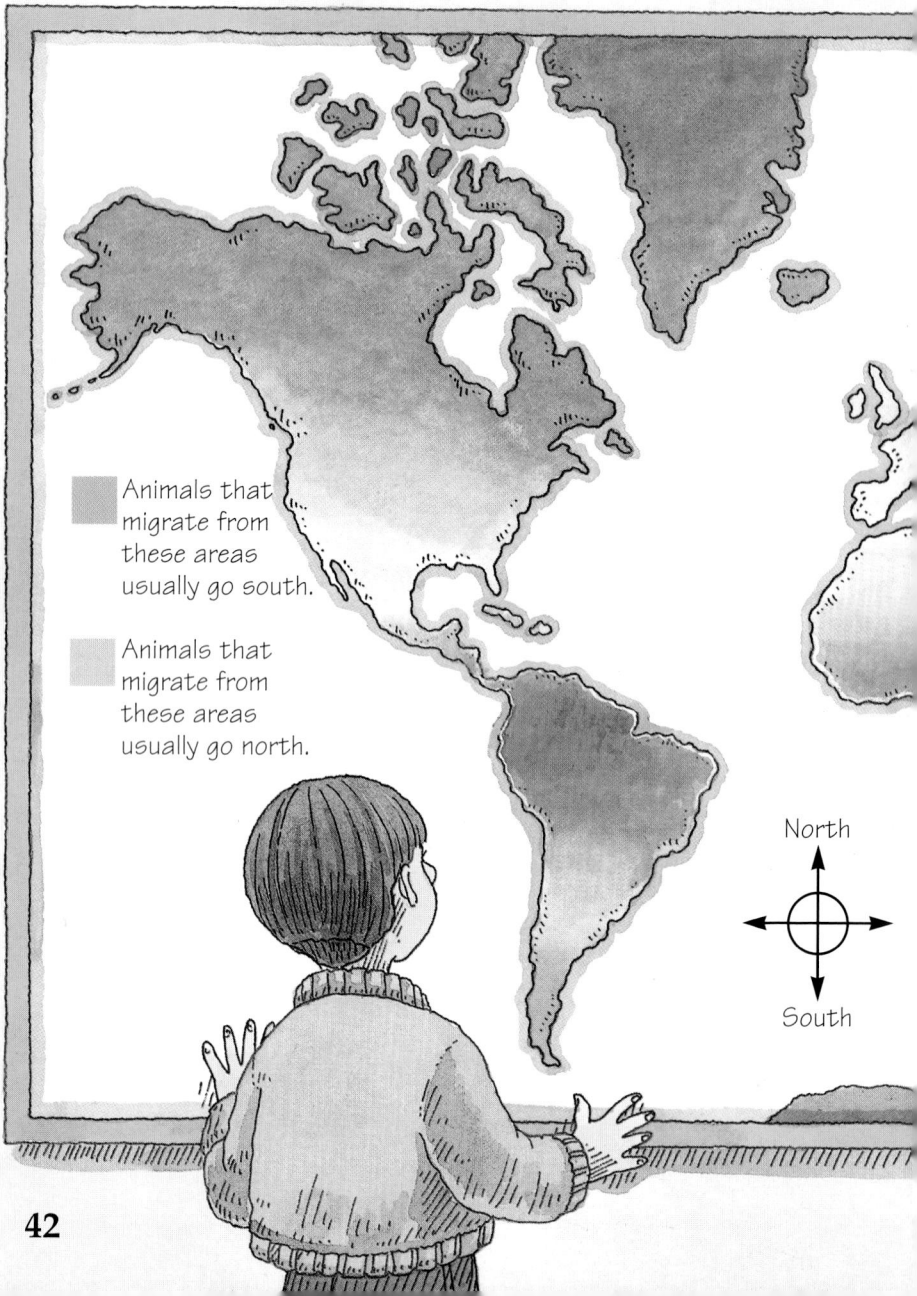

But wherever winter weather comes,
animals must find ways to survive.

So what do animals *do* in winter?

Some animals travel.

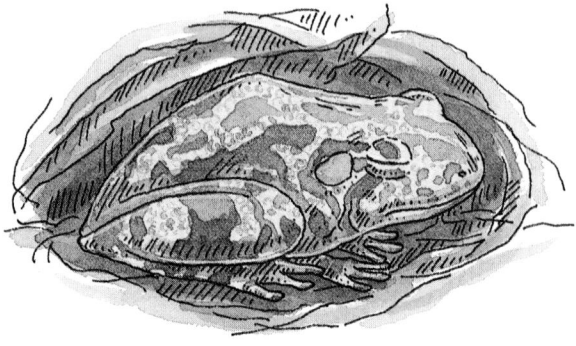

Some animals sleep.

Some animals hide.

Some animals change color.

Humans also live in places that get very cold.

What do *they* do in winter?

A few people migrate to where it is warm.
Most do not.
They spend more time inside their warm houses.
They wear extra layers of clothing.
They have fun in the ice and snow!

Index

ants, 31
Arctic tern, 11
bats, 22
bears, 24
beavers, 32–33
bees, 30
birds, 8–11
caterpillars, 34
chipmunks, 26–27
cocoon, 34
crickets, 35
feathers, 39
foxes, 39–40
frogs, 23
fur color, 36–38
groundhogs, 18–21
hibernate, 18–27
humans, 45–47
migrate, 5–17, 42–43
monarch butterflies, 12–13
Northern Hemisphere, 41
ptarmigan, 39
raccoons, 25
reindeer, 14–15
robins, 9
snails, 23
snakes, 23
snowshoe rabbits, 38
Southern Hemisphere, 41
squirrels, 23, 28–29
turtles, 23
warblers, 10
weasels, 37
whales, 16–17